The Preamble
The Spirit of America

We the People

insure domestic Tranquility, provide for the common
and our Posterity, do ordain and establish this Consti

Article I

Lorin Driggs

Reader Consultants

Cheryl Norman Lane, M.A.Ed.
Classroom Teacher
Chino Valley Unified School District

Jennifer M. Lopez, M.S.Ed., NBCT
Teacher Specialist—History/Social Studies
Norfolk Public Schools

iCivics Consultants

Emma Humphries, Ph.D.
Chief Education Officer

Taylor Davis, M.T.
Director of Curriculum and Content

Natacha Scott, MAT
Director of Educator Engagement

Publishing Credits

Rachelle Cracchiolo, M.S.Ed., *Publisher*
Emily R. Smith, M.A.Ed., *VP of Content Development*
Véronique Bos, *Creative Director*
Dona Herweck Rice, *Senior Content Manager*
Dani Neiley, *Associate Content Specialist*
Fabiola Sepulveda, *Series Designer*

Image Credits: pp.4–5 Library of Congress [LC-USZ62-995]; pp.6–9 Bill
Greenhead; p.10 Library of Congress; p.12 (right) Godot13 via Wikicommons;
p.15 Library of Congress [LC-USZ62-77909]; p.16 (left) Executive Office of the
President of the United States; p.16 (middle) Department of Defense. Department
of the Navy. Naval Photographic Center; p.17 USAGov; p.19 North Wind Picture
Archives/Alamy; p.20 Everett Collection Historical/Alamy; p.25 Michael Ventura /
Alamy Stock Photo; pp.28–29 Architect of the Capitol; all other images from iStock
and/or Shutterstock

Library of Congress Cataloging-in-Publication Data

Names: Driggs, Lorin, author.
Title: The preamble : the spirit of America / Lorin Driggs.
Description: Huntington Beach, CA : Teacher Created Materials, [2021] |
  Includes index. | Audience: Grades 2-3 (provided by Teacher Created
  Materials) | Description based on print version record and CIP data
  provided by publisher; resource not viewed.
Identifiers: LCCN 2020016311 (print) | LCCN 2020016312 (ebook) | ISBN
  9781087619392 (ebook) | ISBN 9781087605159 (paperback) |
  Subjects: LCSH: United States. Constitution. Preamble--Juvenile literature. |
  Constitutional law--United States--Juvenile literature. | Civics--Juvenile
  literature.
Classification: LCC KF4550.Z9 (ebook) | LCC KF4550.Z9 D75 2021 (print) | DDC
  342.7302--dc23
LC record available at https://lccn.loc.gov/2020016311

5482 Argosy Avenue
Huntington Beach, CA 92649-1039
www.tcmpub.com

ISBN 978-1-0876-0515-9

Table of Contents

1787

The war with England was over. The United States of America was a free nation. But soon, the country was in trouble. The government was weak. It had very little money. People were unhappy. Something had to be done. If not, the new nation would fail.

In May 1787, George Washington traveled to Philadelphia, Pennsylvania. Other leaders joined him there. Their job was to fix what wasn't working. The nation's future was in their hands.

They met for four months. They talked. They wrote. They argued. They rewrote. Finally, they agreed.

Washington and other leaders in 1787

Jump into Fiction

A Big Day in Philadelphia

The line is so long, Mom. This will take forever! Can't we just go to the park instead?

VOTE HERE

VOTE HERE

Voting is my right under the Constitution. It's an important part of being a citizen of the United States. I don't care how long I have to wait in line.

What's the Constitution?

Why is voting important?

What's the big deal?

You have a lot of questions, my son. The answers are right here in Philadelphia. I will show you.

Back to Nonfiction

Words to Live By

"We the People of the United States..."

Today, there are 50 states in the United States. In 1787, there were only 13 states. Twelve of those states sent people to help write the **Constitution**. Yes, those writers wanted the best for their states. But more importantly, they wanted the best for the people of the United States. If they did not do a good job, all the people would suffer.

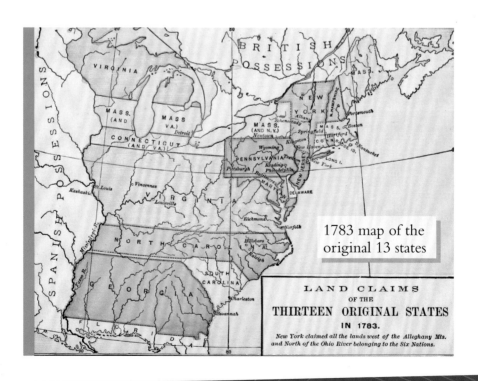

1783 map of the original 13 states

LAND CLAIMS
OF THE
THIRTEEN ORIGINAL STATES
IN 1783.

New York claimed all the lands west of the Alleghany Mts. and North of the Ohio River belonging to the Six Nations.

We now call the writers of the Constitution the "Framers." They created the **framework** for our government. All the U.S. laws are based on it. It tells people what it means to be a **citizen**.

The **Preamble** is an introduction. It gives hints about what is in the Constitution. It shows what the Framers thought was most important.

The Day Franklin Cried

Benjamin Franklin was the oldest person to sign the Constitution. He was 81 years old. He was not healthy and needed help signing. Tears of joy streamed down his face as he signed his name.

Think **and** Talk

Why did Ben Franklin cry? For what reasons do we cry in addition to sadness?

"in Order to form a more perfect Union..."

The *United* States of America is a **union** of states. A union is a group working together. The goal is to help all people. One government unites the states. It is called the **federal** government.

There seemed to be no union at all in 1787. Money was a big problem. Each state could make its own money. And the federal government could not collect **taxes**. It couldn't pay an army. It couldn't pay the president. It couldn't pay other workers. It couldn't do much at all.

state-specific money from the 1700s

George Washington was president from 1789 to 1797.

The United States was failing. The Constitution saved it. The Constitution kept the federal government in charge. The federal government makes the country's money. It collects taxes to pay for all sorts of projects, services, and workers.

What can states do? What can the federal government do? What rights do people have? The Constitution has the answers. It makes a stronger union.

Spending, Then and Now

In 1792, the U.S. government spent just over $5 million (around $136 million in today's money). In 2020, it spent $6.5 trillion.

"establish Justice..."

The Framers thought a lot about **justice**. Justice means fairness. Americans were not treated fairly by England. That's why they fought to be free.

The Constitution takes justice very seriously. It has rules about what is legal and what is not. It explains how courts work. It lists rights that all citizens have. For example, citizens have the right to say what they think. This is called freedom of speech. Citizens have the right to practice any religion they choose. They also have the right to practice no religion. This is called freedom of religion.

People use their right to free speech.

An American Indian man is stopped from voting.

The Constitution says national laws must have the same meaning in every state. They must be fair for all citizens. It does not matter what job someone has. It does not matter where someone lives. It does not matter how much money someone earns. Justice is for all people.

Left Out

The Preamble did not give justice to enslaved people or American Indians. They did not have equal rights. One of those rights was the power to vote. In most states long ago, only white men who owned land could vote. No woman could vote.

The Framers wanted to make sure that no person or no part of the government had too much power. That was also part of being fair.

The Constitution divided the government into three parts. These parts are called *branches*. The three branches have different jobs, but they are equal. No branch is more important than the others. They must work together. One branch makes laws. This is **Congress**. Every state sends representatives to Congress. One branch makes sure the laws are followed. The president is in charge of this branch. The third branch decides what laws mean. This is the system of courts. Even today, new laws cannot break the rules of the Constitution.

Legislative
(makes laws)

Executive
(carries out laws)

Judicial
(interprets laws)

3 BRANCHES *of* U.S. GOVERNMENT

★ ★   ★ ★

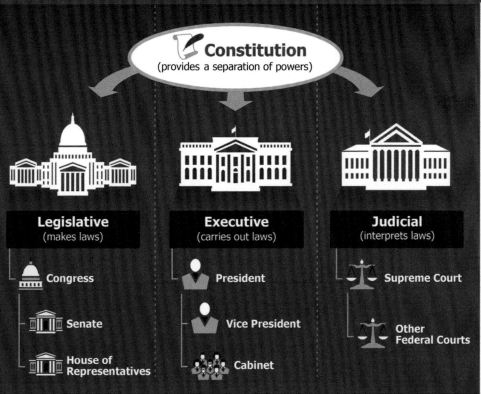

Constitution
(provides a separation of powers)

Legislative
(makes laws)

- Congress
- Senate
- House of Representatives

Executive
(carries out laws)

- President
- Vice President
- Cabinet

Judicial
(interprets laws)

- Supreme Court
- Other Federal Courts

What To Say?

One issue the new U.S. **Senate** had to solve was what to call the president. Suggestions included: "His Elective Highness" and "Most Illustrious and Excellent President." Both titles embarrassed President Washington. So, the Senate chose "Mr. President." When a woman is elected, it will be "Madam President."

"insure domestic Tranquility..."

In 1787, the United States was in trouble. The war had been expensive. People were in debt. They were struggling. Farmers faced problems. A lot of them had borrowed money to grow extra food during the war. They owed that money back. Most farmers couldn't pay what they owed. Sometimes, their land was taken from them. Some people were put in jail for their debts. There were **riots** and other acts of violence. The weak government had no power to act. The Framers wanted to make sure these problems could be solved.

The Constitution changed things. The government could pay for the costs of war. It had the power to deal with riots and violence in the states. **Domestic** tranquility in the phrase above means peace at home. The Constitution made this possible.

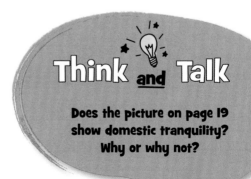

Think and Talk

Does the picture on page 19 show domestic tranquility? Why or why not?

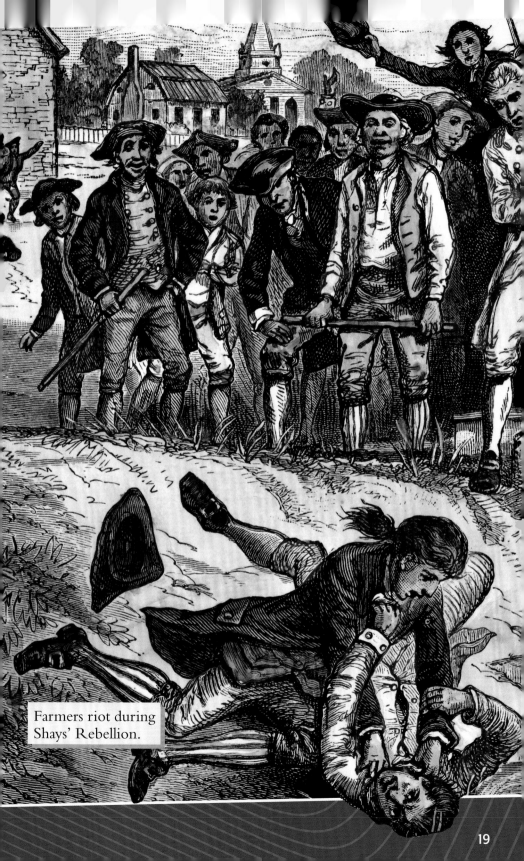

Farmers riot during Shays' Rebellion.

The Framers also argued over the best way to keep the new nation safe. What if another country attacked? The United States had no army. The federal government was almost helpless. It could not afford to buy weapons. It could not afford to pay soldiers or buy uniforms. Money wasn't the only problem. Rules about who should be in charge of defending the nation were unclear. Before then, each state was in charge of its own defense.

The Framers had to find a way to keep the entire nation safe. So, they put the president in charge of the armed forces. They called the position the "commander in chief." But they didn't want the president to have too much power. So, they wrote that Congress shared that power. They made it so that only Congress can send the country to war.

President Franklin Roosevelt signs a notice of war from Congress.

members of the
armed forces

"promote the general Welfare..."

What should a government do for its people? How should it take care of them? The Framers thought about these things. They used the words "general welfare" in the Preamble. That means the health, comfort, and happiness of the people.

Taxes pay for roads and bridges.

People need clean water and air. They need safe roads and bridges. People need laws that protect and treat them fairly. They need a government that works for them. These are just some examples. The government can do these things because it can pass laws. It can spend money to get things done. It has money to spend because it can collect taxes. These powers are written into the Constitution.

Think and Talk

What else, if anything, do you think your government should do for you?

> *"and secure the Blessings of Liberty to ourselves and our Posterity, do ordain and establish this Constitution for the United States of America."*

Freedom was a major reason people came to what is now the United States. Later, these people fought a war to be free of English rule. The Framers of the Constitution thought a lot about what **liberty** would mean in the new nation.

The Constitution is more than 230 years old. The Framers could not have imagined the world of today. Still, the government they designed survives. It works for the world we know now. The United States remains a nation of laws. Americans are still free.

When people do not follow the laws of the Constitution, they may have to go to court.

People change and countries change. The Constitution was a guide in the past. It is a guide for now and the future too. As long as people follow it, the United States will survive. As long as people respect it, Americans will remain free.

On Display

People can view the original Constitution. It is in Washington, DC. It is the oldest written constitution of any major world government.

Changing the Constitution

The original Constitution was short—only four pages long. It was written by hand. It is now much longer. Why? The Framers were very smart. They thought about the future. They included a way to change the Constitution.

Changing the Constitution is not easy. It can take a long time. First, Congress has to approve the change. Then, three-fourths of the states have to vote to approve it. There are 50 states today. That means that 38 states would have to agree to a change.

the Bill of Rights

Constitutional changes are called **amendments**. So far, there have been 27 amendments. The first 10 amendments were added in 1791. They appear in a section called the Bill of Rights.

A woman votes for president in 1920.

Freedom and Rights Granted

People have recommended more than 11,000 amendments! Only 27 suggestions have passed. For example, the Thirteenth Amendment passed in 1865. It ended slavery. In 1920, the Nineteenth Amendment passed. It gave women the legal right to vote.

The Spirit of a Nation

What did the Framers hope for? The Preamble tells us. In just 52 words, the Framers laid out the rest of the document. They wrote about what was important. They wrote about how the country would run.

The Preamble tells what the United States stood for in 1787. Americans still believe in those **ideals**. They believe that people should be free. They believe that the states are united. They believe in justice for all people. They want peace within the country. They want all citizens to succeed. They want liberty, now and in the future.

The Preamble is the only part of the Constitution that can't be changed. It is the spirit of the Constitution. It is the spirit of the United States of America.

Think *and* Talk

Choose someone in this picture. What do you think they might be thinking or saying?

Glossary

amendments—changes made to laws or legal documents

citizen—a person who has legal rights in a country

Congress—made up of the Senate and the House of Representatives, it is the branch of the government that makes laws

Constitution—the basic framework of the United States government

domestic—relating to your own country

federal—relating to the main or central government of a nation

framework—the basic structure or ideas for something

ideals—ideas or standards of excellence or perfection

justice—fair and equal treatment under the law

liberty—freedom

Preamble—the introduction to the U.S. Constitution that summarizes the reasons for the Constitution

riots—violent demonstrations by people who are upset about things

Senate—the smaller of the two groups that make up the U.S. Congress

taxes—money that people and businesses pay to support the government

union—a group of states or people working together to help one another

Index

Civics in Action

The Preamble tells what the United States stands for. It lets people know the values that are important to the country. You can write a preamble for your classroom. It will let other students know what values are important to your class.

1. Make a list of what is important in the Preamble to the U.S. Constitution.

2. Make a list of what is important in your classroom.

3. Draft a preamble for your classroom. Model the structure of your writing after the Preamble to the U.S. Constitution.

4. Make a poster with your preamble. Include pictures that explain your wording.